Taking the Biscuit:
My Experience of Being Married to a Sex Addict

Introduction:

Sex addiction is a controversial subject for some, but the simple truth is that there are people who do self-destructive things related to sex that they feel they cannot control. When a person chooses to have sex with someone they find physically repulsive, it's difficult to argue that they didn't want to control their behavior. When someone masturbates so often they hurt themselves, it is clearly compulsive. My goal is not to persuade you that sex addiction is a *bona fide* disorder. I simply am here to tell my story. Monster or sick? You decide.

A note about this book: I worked hard to keep this book short and succinct. Is there more I could say? You bet. But in the interest of respecting your time, I asked myself whether a particular point was necessary, and if the answer was not a resounding "yes!", I cut it. I want you to know my story. I want this disease to come out into the light.

A note about our children: Our children are growing up in an era where we cannot protect them. They are exposed to far too many things, far too early. The current crop of 40-year-olds grew up in an era before the Internet. Despite this, many of today's 40-year-old sex addicts say that they started with the underwear models in JC Penney catalogs.

Today, much more graphic images are easily available, and depict sex in a way that is entirely contradictory to healthy sexual intimacy. The most common age that sex addicts say their addiction began is 12 years old. I purposely did not restrict this book to the 18+ age group. If unhealthy behaviors start at age 12, adolescents need to learn to distinguish what is healthy and unhealthy before that. By age 18, most sex addicts have been "using" their drug of choice for many years. Sex addiction develops early in life, because it's in adolescence that we experiment with various coping mechanisms and our developing bodies. We do not have the luxury of waiting until our brains are more fully developed. Anorexia, bulimia, substance abuse, smoking, and porn use most commonly begin well before 18 years of age.

My Extreme Gratitude:

I am extremely grateful for all the love and support I have received from others, especially my family, long-term friends, extended family, church family, "rehab spouses' day" friend, and my COSA family. In addition, I am grateful to my employees who endured the hardships of a rudderless ship and kept the place humming through the bad times with their dedication and loyalty.

Table of Contents

Down the Rabbit Hole

The end of this month marks 5 years since the crazy weekend that spun my world into oblivion. That was the weekend that threw me down the rabbit hole into a world that I never imagined. That weekend, visions of the white rabbit and Alice in her little blue dress swirled in my head as I listened with horror to the filth and drivel that came from my husband's mouth. Ironically, it was Memorial Day weekend; truly a weekend to remember.

When did it start? Did it start when I saw my husband in the breakroom at lunchtime and noticed how haggard he looked? Did it start when I put my hand on his cheek and told him he should go home and rest, he's been traveling so much and he was clearly wiped out? Or did it start days before, when he knew that when he returned home, there was no more hiding his STD (sexually-transmitted disease) before I would discover it? Perhaps he hadn't slept, fretting on one hand that I would surely leave him; and concerned on the other hand that he was permanently damaged by a rash that would not quit.

What I do know is that when I returned home that Friday night, he asked me to come into our bedroom because he had something to tell me. I followed him in, knowing in my gut that he was clearly upset about something, and that I would not like what it was. He lay down on the bed and said, "I slept with someone. Again. I was not drunk this time."

The reference to the prior infidelity was when he claimed to have contracted an STD from a blow job. That was 5 years prior. At that point in time, we had been together for 17 years. I considered leaving him but he spent 6 months saying "I'm sorry," and working hard to convince me to give him another chance. So I did give him another chance. In fact, I was so gullible, that I felt our marriage and commitment to each other was stronger than ever. Clearly that was not the case.

I sat there, stunned. I asked who the person was. He said he didn't know her name. That really threw me for a loop. I didn't believe that at all. I asked again. He wasn't prepared at all for that question, and continued to assert that he didn't know her name. He said, "I guess you want me to leave now." I said I didn't understand. And this went on, and on.

I left the room. I poured some wine.

I checked on our two 10 and 8-year old kids, happily watching Disney in the living room.

I then announced to him, "We will get through this. This is just another adventure for us to go through." I don't think I knew what I was saying, exactly. Except we were soulmates, a couple that everyone thought would be together forever, and had already been together by this time for 22 years. It was, in fact, half the amount of time I had been on this earth.

I don't recall what else was said on Friday night; but I do know that I discovered no more information from him other than no, despite my suspicions, it wasn't some man that he hooked up with, and wasn't telling me "her" name because it was a guy. In college, people had assumed he was gay. He insisted that it was not a guy and that no, he didn't know her name.

That night, he sacked out, snoring. I'm sure he had had a lot to drink as well.

I, however, had just picked up the burden that he had been carrying, and sleep eluded me. I tried to sleep on our daughter's top bunk bed, but I decided in the end to get up and pace the floors. I checked his cell phone. And there it was; calls to many phone numbers that I could Google. The calls to hookers had started with the first city in which he changed planes. Google the phone number, and you even see the woman's photo. *Of course!* That's why he couldn't *remember* her name! He didn't know her name because she was a *hooker!*

The truth is, however, more bizarre than that.

The next morning, in the privacy of our bedroom, I announced to him that I was upset because he was still lying to me. He looked me in the eye, and said, "You're right. I'm still lying to you." At which point, to my surprise, he unzipped his pants and whipped out his <bleep> to show me his rash. Now, this was even more bizarre. I was immediately thrown. It was so wrong and warped. Was I his mother now? Did he think I would be as concerned about his rash as he was? Frankly, I didn't want to see it, although he was clearly concerned that the rash was still there and seemed afraid it had moved permanently into his life. I, on the other hand, was more concerned about bigger things!

I didn't know how to respond. On one hand, he didn't answer the most important question to me: who was the woman he was with? Clearly a hooker. Instead, he did something so bizarre, I wondered what in the world I should think or do after that happened. I opted for escape. I told him I needed to get our 8-year-old daughter to her appointment, because the pediatrician said they could see her that morning.

And here's the next bizarre series of events that was happening concurrently: our daughter had been having pain in her "private parts". As was the agreement that she and I had, she knew it was up to her to tell me when the pain was bad enough that she needed to go to the doctor. She informed me the night before that it was time to go to the doctor.

So I got dressed, gathered up my things, and got in the car with our daughter. I have no idea how I managed that.

We arrived at the pediatrician's office, and described the pain she was feeling in her "private parts". The pediatrician said she would do a test to see if our daughter had a urinary tract infection, but would give us antibiotics to treat it, because it took a long time to confirm a bacterial infection. She assured me that this was common in girls her age. However, after the doctor left the room, it slowly dawned on me that, crazy as it sounds, this is really odd timing for our daughter to have some sort of infection down there, at the same time that I had already seen evidence of an infection on her father. My stomach did extreme acrobatics at the thought. I decided not to mention anything to the doctor. I knew I could go outside and discuss it privately; however, I wasn't sure if the doctor would be compelled to do something like report it to Social Services. I did not want to take that chance; and I wasn't sure if I was making some gross error in judgment. What if that made no sense, somehow, and it caused us to get thrown into the system? I was definitely entering new territory, and I was drowning because I didn't know up from down. I was down the rabbit hole, and what I knew as true appeared to be the reverse of what was real.

Instead of recounting the rest of the weekend play by play, here are the facts as they unfolded. They unfolded in a jumbled, garbled way, throughout the rest of the weekend.

Facts:

- When I confronted him about the prostitutes, he still claimed the un-named woman was not a hooker, but a certain person who we both knew. He said he was humiliated to admit he slept with that particular woman, because he felt she was physically repulsive, allegedly, because she was "fat".
- He also told me he had anal sex with her as well. That was an image I wish I had never had! Why would he tell me that? It was as if he were in a stupor himself; in shock and not aware at all of who he was speaking to.
- I asked for proof that he slept with the woman he knew, because I believed he was too ashamed to admit that he "paid for sex" (his words - he said "I don't *have* to *pay for sex*"). He showed me that he told her via LinkedIn that he had an STD and she

needed to get checked out. She replied, "Thanks for the heads up."

- After I confronted him with the evidence of the prostitutes, however, it turned out he was with a hooker on Sunday night, a different hooker on Monday night, and then the woman he knew from our industry on Tuesday night.
- There is no way to know, by the way, whether he gave that STD to the industry colleague from one of the prostitutes, or the other way around. Despite that, he accused her of giving the STD to him.
- Later, when I asked him how often he used a condom with all of the women he slept with, he told me it was less than 50% of the time.
- I went to the only clinic open that Saturday of Memorial Day weekend, and am very grateful to Planned Parenthood that they were able to assist. They gave me medicine for chlamydia, prior to waiting for the test results to return, and also a rapid HIV test to see if I had the virus. However, they were very clear that I would not be able to be sure that I was HIV free until after 6 months had passed. Believe me, that was a *long* wait.
- I asked him at one point whether he had had sex with any of these women more than once. He replied, "all of them." I was stunned. I said you kept seeing all of them more than once? He said that he had sex several times each night with each person he slept with. Three times in the case of the last person that he had had sex with. When I clarified my question, that I wanted to know if he kept on hooking up with one person each time that he saw them, he told me yes, that was true with one person. Then he told me who that was. I asked how

many times. He said 7 separate occasions. I asked why it stopped. He said it was getting weird - he didn't want it to become a regular thing.

- Note: once I found out who this person was, I realized (1) he had previously told me a ton of information about the companies and people she worked with, unabashedly and unashamed that he had gotten that information while in bed with her and (2) he had purposefully sent me over to meet her at her trade show booth 6 months previously. Why did he want me to go and meet her? Make the point to her that he really did have a wife? Some sick satisfaction in seeing his two 'women' interacting? To make her jealous? Whatever the reason, it was so entirely in disregard of *my* feelings, I am sickened.

- On Sunday night, I told him to leave. He went to a hotel.

- We told the kids that Daddy was moving out. He said that we had been fighting so much he needed to leave. That was a little odd to tell the kids; we had rarely fought prior to that weekend, so I didn't want them to think that a simple day or two of fighting is what leads to Daddy moving out. I told them the truth, as best that I could, by explaining that it wasn't that we were fighting. It was that Daddy had done something, and it had hurt Mommy's feelings. We needed to have some time apart to work through it. They were upset, but they seemed to be reassured that we both loved them, and that they would still get to see Daddy.

- One of the hookers he chose used the *same name as our daughter*. That haunts me to this day. Our daughter's name is VERY unique. What type of father chooses a hooker with the same unique name as his daughter?

- A couple days after he told me about his STD, I left for my brother's and sister-in-law's house to get some distance from the situation and to think. Before I left, my 8-year-old daughter asked me, "Not to let Daddy hurt her." That stopped me in my tracks. I asked her what she meant. She looked scared. She said, "Daddy hurt your feelings. I don't want him to hurt me either." I reassured her that he wouldn't and then I confronted him about what she said. When he realized what I was accusing him of, he went berserk. Crying, he claimed that that was completely unfair, and verbally attacked me for even thinking that he was capable of that. What good parent can ignore their daughter's words of "Don't let Daddy hurt me" under this particular set of circumstances?

- A couple months later, when our daughter complained again of pain in her privates, despite the antibiotics, and while her father was away at a rehab facility for sex addiction, I took her back to the pediatrician's office. This time, however, I took the pediatrician into a separate room and told her I wanted our daughter tested for every STD known to man. I wanted to make sure that this recurring pain in her urinary tract area had nothing to do with her father. All tests came back clean, thankfully.

- Risking being reported to Social Services, I also told the elementary school guidance counselor that I wanted her to talk to our daughter to see if she believed there was any reason for concern. She did talk to our daughter, and concluded that nothing justified further investigation.

- I backed off, but have been vigilant ever since.
- Oh, and last, but not least, by the grace of God, I am indeed, HIV-free.

How It All Began

Democrat or Republican? Meeting over a toilet. Soulmates. The good, the bad, and the ugly. Let me take you back in time to the place where it all began. As the song goes, this was summertime in northern Michigan. There were sandbars and campfires, and it even was the same year of 1989.

Now, I knew better. My parents had met in this idyllic place, and that marriage was a rocky one. I even said to Trevor at the time that this was simply a summer romance, because my parents met at the same place, and their relationship didn't last. However, we often do things that are not good for us, and despite multiple warning signs, I looked the other way.

The good.
The good things were that we could talk forever. I felt understood. I felt I could tell him anything, and that he truly listened. He would respond with something that made it clear that he had heard what I said. He was willing to do different, crazy things, and we seemed to have just about all the same interests. We liked similar books, similar music, and held the same points of view on most things. There were very few things that we didn't see eye to eye on. Most of all, we simply enjoyed hanging out

together and talking.

We were both optimistic and got excited about ideas. We could talk forever about ideas. I think in a lot of ways, I was missing the relationship that I had had growing up with my brother Don. Don and I became estranged when I was 19, so when I met Trevor at age 22, I felt that I had someone in my life again who loved talking about different ideas. Things that I thought about and liked to talk about. Like Tesla, for example. My brother Don talked a lot about Nikolai Tesla, and I talked to Trevor about that and he liked talking about things like that as well. I think that for the most part, it's what caused me to fall in love with him. The ability to talk forever and carry on conversations about ideas and theories and well, life! It was a piece of home, it was how life was during late nights in the kitchen of my cozy family home, talking to my mother, or to my brother, or maybe to both, about all those ideas and dreams and "what if" hypotheses.

My own parents divorced when I was 3 years old. As a **high schooler**, I talked a lot with each of them about why their marriage didn't work. Each of them agreed, separately, that poor communication was the problem. They simply felt they couldn't communicate effectively with each other. That's why I put a lot of importance on that in my own relationships. With Trevor, I felt like I had achieved a deeper level of communication than I ever had before, even deeper than in the relationship that I would describe as my first love, which was with a Brit, who had a distinctively different cultural background than mine.

I also realize that the way that we met was pretty important. My friend threw a party at her parents' house when they weren't home. She had been very nervous about it, but decided to do it anyway. Then some drunk person shattered the coffee pot in the kitchen. She was beside herself. The next thing that I heard was that the toilet was clogged. I decided to see if I could fix it before she knew about it. As I looked at it, Trevor popped up beside me and said, "Did you know that toilets drain the opposite way in Australia?" With that comment, and also the goofy Aussie slouch hat that he had on his head, I recognized a person who was not afraid to express himself. I had always been attracted to that type of person. What's more, he stayed and helped me fix the broken toilet before my friend could get upset about it. What a sweet thing to do, right?

For years after that, I joked that we met over a toilet. It was, in fact, true.

Also, he didn't kiss me until much later, and even then, before he kissed me, he made a point of asking if I were "a Democrat or a Republican". I thought it was an endearing thing that he needed to know that before he kissed me. It implied that he had other standards for who I was, as opposed to just how I looked. We laughed about it and apparently, I answered the right way.

The bad.
There were definitely warning signs. One of my brothers was at that same party. He met him too. What I thought were quirky and charming traits, he thought were oddball and downright slimy traits. Later, after getting to know Trevor's family, Trevor's own sister asked me what I was doing with him, because "you're so nice, and he's so mean". I told her that she was wrong! I said that because

she was his sister, they had some type of rivalry. I wrote it off as inconsequential! Ironically, it was in stark contrast to the good relationship I had with my own brother. Was it already too late at that point? Had I already made up my mind? Was I going to ignore all the warning signs?

Other people didn't seem to think he was arrogant. I think. He had friends in any case, but looking back, people just seemed to think he was fun to hang around. I can't really say that his friends, of which there were not very many, would have described him as kind or generous. In fact, he had the nick name of "T-bone". So the T is for Trevor, and the rest is for...?

Then the ugly hit.
This was the time that I should have run for the hills, licked my wounds, and started again. One evening after seeing each other each day for 2 weeks, he announced, "I can't see you tomorrow. My girlfriend is coming into town."

I mean, it was completely bizarre. I asked him to explain. He then said, "I mean, I'm going to break up with her, but she and her family came here to vacation and I will tell her tomorrow that I'm with you." Now, not only had he neglected to tell me that he had a girlfriend, this family traveled from 7 hours away to spend the week where their daughter's boyfriend was. He didn't have the decency to tell her ahead of time that he was going to shatter her dreams of an enjoyable summer vacation, nor the decency to stick it out with her since he screwed things up so badly. His way of dealing with the situation was to blurt out what I wanted to hear the day before his girlfriend of 2 years arrived. He did actually follow through and break up with her. He spent that week with me, and presumably, that girl and her family had one sucky week where they were somewhere that they didn't want to be.

Taking the Biscuit

It wasn't until my journey through the addiction and recovery community that I learned that the thoughts I let into my brain affect me as much as the food that I eat. The idea of *emotional nutrition* was not something that had ever occurred to me. If you will forgive the analogy, gorging on delicious, fresh-baked, lumps of flour, lard and sugar, slathered with butter, is how I got into this mess. *Naive?* All my life I'd been told that I am unusually naive. My childhood friend used to often say this to me: "For someone so smart, you are so dumb." I believed just about anything that people told me.

Hand me a biscuit, tell me that its nutritious, and that I can eat it and only it for the rest of my life, and I will believe you. I took that biscuit. I didn't question whether it was nutritious. I believed that what I was being fed was good for me, even though it was clearly too good to be true.

Yes, I took the biscuit, and we married in our mid-20s.

Trying To Get Pregnant

We started a business together after I left my corporate job. Life seemed pretty easy and stress-free at the time. We lived in a beautiful home, in a beautiful place, and the world seemed full of promise. We had lunch together at the picnic table in the backyard, and for me, the joy of creating something that I could be proud of. I had wanted to start a business in order to make something great. Knowing that I was contributing to something that would become bigger than myself, and knowing that I was building something lasting, was very fulfilling to me.

Also, I had just turned 30 years old. It seemed like a good time to have a baby. Ok, so you know where I am headed. Working hard to have a baby with a sex addict does not sound like a difficult thing at all! However, as with many things in life, this disease of sex addiction is just dripping with irony. I consider myself gruesomely fortunate, in a sense, because he was hyper-sexual, and not "sexually anorexic." Ironically, many sex addicts refuse to have sex with their spouses and are deemed sexually "anorexic". If I can digress, perhaps those are the ones with better consciences, because they know that they might have an STD, or at least that they actually feel some sort of guilt about their deception that is causing them to not want to have sex with their spouses. It's just a thought.

In any case, Trevor was ready and willing for the task. This lasted for a total of 19 months, during which I purchased many, many ovulation tests and became increasingly frustrated by my husband's refusal to change any of his pot-smoking, drinking, or hot tub habits. This was even after the tests came back showing that his swimmers swam 95% less than other males his age. Yes, he was shooting blanks and didn't care to change his actions to improve the odds.

Actually, that was an ongoing trait for him. I had often told him that he wanted so many things in life, yet didn't take the actions required to achieve those things. He expected to get good grades without studying, have a great body without exercising. This was no different.

I should feel pretty indignant about how willing he was for the task, especially after we went to the first prenatal visit together.

The nurse asked me a series of questions about my heritage, with the purpose of deciding what prenatal tests I should be given. When it came to talking about the HIV test, I laughed and said I had been together with my husband for 9 years, and I didn't think I needed an HIV test.

Trevor spoke up. He said, "Honey, I think you should get the test."

It felt like the room tilted on its axis a little bit. I said, "Do you know what you are saying?"

He said, "No, I mean, it's a good idea, you've never been tested for HIV."

I said, "I don't think I need to be tested."

The nurse promptly cut the discussion off, getting up to leave the room and saying, "Well, that settles it. We will do the test."

After she left, I grilled him. He didn't budge from his assertion that it's simply a good idea and that there was nothing behind his comment other than that. I grilled him some more after we got home. For at least 3 days, I grilled him. He would not budge from his protests that he simply thought it was a good idea.

In retrospect, I'm sure that he was extremely relieved when the test came back negative. After the rabbit hole experience of his confession of hookers and one-night stands, he confessed that he started seeing hookers at least as early as after I became pregnant with our first child. He said he had been angry at me that I had wanted to have so much sex in order to get pregnant, and that after I did become pregnant and the sex was less frequent, he felt like he had been used. So this was somehow justification to go out and do whatever he wanted, regardless of the consequences.

Actually, doesn't every addict make some crazy justification to go out and feed their addiction? This was no different.

The truth is, even during my early twenties and in the first years that we were living together in New York City, I kept getting vaginal infections. One of them was from trichomoniasis. The nurse told me that "trich" was only contracted through sex. I told Trevor, who had been my boyfriend at that time for over 2 years. He said, he must have gotten it before he started dating me. Because we were so close and I really couldn't believe that he was cheating on me, I bought it. It didn't even cross my mind that anyone I knew, let alone my boyfriend, liked to visit hookers. For that reason, years later, I still didn't suspect anything even though he was gone so often and for so long allegedly "fly-fishing", that my friends nick-named me the "fly-fishing widow."

Spinning Out Of Control

Prior to the big day of "discovery", where I learned about Trevor's secret life, there were warning signs that something was wrong. Intuitively, for years I felt constant anxiety that there was a time bomb ticking and that something was going to blow up. I suspected things would blow up for us financially, so I devoted an exorbitant amount of time and energy to making sure that didn't happen.

He'd say things like "I'm jealous. You get to go to Michigan and I don't." That would be understandable if it were coming from a teenager. In this case, the reason I was going to Michigan was for my aunt's 80th birthday party, which happened 1 year after my mother passed away. This was a bittersweet, emotional trip for me, because I missed my mom so much. He knew we didn't have the money to fly all four of us there. Yet, he made the declaration that he was jealous, and said it in a way that made it clear he was angry. He then walked away. End of discussion. Basically, it was an "I'm-angry-at-you-wife-and-you-suck"-type of Hallmark moment.

Then there was the comment, "There's something wrong," he'd said in response to my request that for my Mother's Day present that year, I have a night away from it all in a local hotel room. I was getting up at 4 am to work on the business, taking care of kids starting at 6 am, going to work, getting kids to activities after school, continually getting criticized by him in the evening for not being happy to spend time with him at the end of our work day together, going to bed at 10, awakened at 2 am when he stumbled into bed, and starting it all over again the next morning. "Yes," I replied, "I've told you. I'm exhausted. I feel like everyone needs something from me. The kids need me. The company needs me. You need me. Where do my own needs fit in?"

Crazy man comment number three is this: "I don't care

about life insurance. That's only for your benefit anyway." That little bombshell is something he actually said to me in passing one day. I was working on our budget and saying that he should get rated again now that he had "quit smoking". Well, it's likely that he never quit smoking, isn't it? So his $3,000/yr. life insurance policy for a 40 something aged man wasn't going to go down in premium because he would fail the smoking test. However, instead of admitting his own fault, he claimed that he didn't care about me or the kids after he was gone. Because, of course, how could he care? He would be gone.

Yes, there were several things that I saw that I knew were not right. These are just some examples. While I knew that his thinking was warped, I did not know how deep it ran.

I stayed because I had made a commitment to him. I stayed because my vows were in sickness and in health. And I made the most of it, accepting what I could not change and changing the things that I could. I just didn't know that that I was living the serenity prayer outside of the addiction and recovery community.

Sifting Through The Ashes

After the weekend that Alice followed the white rabbit down the rabbit hole, Trevor decided to go to rehab for sex addiction. I told him at the time that I couldn't guarantee that I would be around after he completed it, and that he shouldn't do it for me. While I didn't want him to expect that it would save our marriage, I'm sure that it was clear in my voice that I was hopeful that it would.

After he returned from his 10-day intensive rehab program

for sex addicts, he attended 90 Sex Addicts Anonymous (SAA) meetings in 90 days. His sobriety plan included doing check-ins with me where we talked about our feelings. During one of these check-ins, he called himself "a liar, a cheat and a thief." I told him I certainly understood the liar and the cheat part of the phrase, but why did he include the word "thief"? He said, "I was a thief because I stole from the family." I asked, did he mean with prostitutes? He said yes. Mind you, prior to that, he said that he had only paid for prostitutes to come and "dance" for him in his hotel room. He claimed they arrived with bodyguards to make sure that they only danced. It was a pretty ridiculous claim. While it probably happened to him at least one disappointing time, he wrote in his recovery workbook that he felt guilty about the prostitutes, and the proof that he had hired the more sexually-satisfying kind of hookers was right there in front of me in the word, "thief." (In fact, this type of "dribbling" out of parts of the truth is extremely common for sex addicts. It is also extremely painful for their partners to experience.)

What did become clear was that as soon as he got into the "bubble" of his addiction, especially while traveling (although not always), he was a different person. People who knew him on the road tell me today that they had no idea he was even married; while people at home who knew us both, believed he was so devoted to me that I must have been making it up that he even looked at another woman. He was leading a double life.

After the first infidelity, when we put hundreds of hours into self-development courses, exploring the importance of integrity, and honesty, he had lied throughout the entire experience. No, I didn't see any reason to believe that this time he would do anything more than deny and lie. And even if he did eventually clean up his act, I didn't think that it would occur while he was with me. He didn't believe I would leave him. If I stayed, he would believe that it wasn't really that big a deal. He already believed it wasn't that big a deal. He didn't think what he did was morally wrong. He believed himself to be a normal red-blooded American man. He felt that it was only wrong because it hurt me. He also knew he didn't want me sleeping with other men. He had no moral compass.

My decision came to me in a flash of clarity one evening when I was at the stove, doing the comforting evening ritual of cooking for my children. It all boiled down to these 3 simple questions:
1. If I stay in this relationship because of money, how am I different from being a prostitute myself?
2. If my mother were still alive, would she want me to stay in this relationship?
3. If my daughter, or my son, came to me in 20 years' time with the circumstances of this relationship, what would I tell them to do?

Those were simple, yet powerful, questions that I asked myself.

So, after 22 years of believing that I had been living with my soulmate, having children with this man, and building a business with him that had grown to over 20 employees, I filed for divorce, thereby stepping off a cliff. It was terrifying. Decades of living in fear of a bomb exploding financially, culminated in this one act. Ironically, I was the one that risked financial ruin, because the bomb that went off, after it had been incessantly ticking for years, was that he was living a secret life.

I knew I would fall, and I didn't know how far, nor whether I would be crippled when I landed. I just knew that I needed to step off that cliff.

* * * * * * * * * * * *

Lyrics from my favorite song of that year of discovery:

Jason Mraz, *The Remedy*, "I Won't Worry My Life Away."

Well, I saw fireworks from the freeway
and behind closed eyes I cannot make them go away
'Cause you were born on the fourth of July, freedom ring
Well, something on the surface, it stinks.
I said something on the surface
well, it kind of makes me nervous
who says that you deserve this?
and what kind of God would serve this?
We will cure this, dirty old disease

If you've gots the poison, I've gots the remedy

The remedy, is the experience.
It is a dangerous liaison
I says the comedy, is that it's serious.
This is a strange enough new play on words
I say the tragedy is how you're gonna spend
the rest of your nights with the light on
So shine the light on all of your friends
Well, it all amounts to nothing in the end.

I won't worry my life away.
I won't worry my life away.

Well, I heard two men talking on the radio
in a cross fire kind of new reality show

Uncovering the ways to plan the next big attack
well, they were counting down the days to stab their
brother in the be right back after this
the unavoidable kiss,
where the minty fresh death breath is sure to outlast this
catastrophe
dance with me,
'cause if you've gots the poison, I've gots the remedy

The remedy, is the experience.
It is a dangerous liaison
I says the comedy is that it's serious.
This is a strange enough new play on words
I say the tragedy is how you're gonna spend
the rest of your nights with the light on
So shine the light on all of your friends
Well, it all amounts to nothing in the end.

I won't worry my life away.
I won't worry my life away.

When I fall in love, I take my time
There's no need to hurry when I'm making up my mind
You can turn off the sun but I'm still gonna shine and I'll
tell you why
Because

The remedy, is the experience.
It is a dangerous liaison
I says the comedy, is that it's serious.
This is a strange enough new play on words
I say the tragedy is how you're gonna spend
the rest of your nights with the light on
So shine the light on all of your friends
Well, it all amounts to nothing in the end.

I won't worry my life away.
I won't worry my life away.
I won't and I won't and I won't [etc.]

How to Assess if Your Sex Addict is Truly Recovering

Yes, he was missing some pretty important character traits that I should have paid attention to. First and foremost, was he a kind person? Did other people like him? How did he treat his own mother? (disdain, fear) How did he treat his sister? (passive aggressive, mean) Yes, culturally, I felt like he was the right mix of intelligence, craziness, spontaneity, adventurousness, and ambition. He wanted to create things and do things, although it was pretty clear I was more ambitious than he ever was. Unlike people who marry for practical reasons or perhaps they feel that it's time or that time is running out, I truly did marry him for love. I felt I would be with him forever, and that our understanding and connection was so deep that it would sustain us. And even if I were wrong, I figured, any problem we encountered we would be able to talk through, because we could communicate well.

That's the flabbergasting thing. I don't understand how I could have a feeling of deep connection with someone who is incapable of connecting with people. He has no capacity for empathy. It's part of his psychological disorder. It's what he said by his own admission, after rehab, and after which the pieces of the puzzle fell into place in my head. It was clear that that was why I had fallen into a habit of continually trying to explain to him what his behavior was doing to other people. For example,

I'd say how would you feel if someone asked you every day to be happy around them regardless of how they actually felt at the time? And he continually would say "I don't know." Or if I said, "Hey, I'm having such a hard time here. Something happened at work and let me tell you about it." After I was finished, he would simply say, "I don't know what to say." It was as if he finally was exhausted from wearing that mask all those years and simply didn't want to pretend he understood. But in the past he always had a response. And I think it might've been to joke around or gosh, I don't know. Why did I feel I had a deep connection with someone who fails to connect? I don't think that I imagined it. I do think he was able to put up a façade of understanding. I don't think that it was obvious he had no capacity for empathy, and I think he worked hard at hiding it. He is a master of manipulation.

Sex addicts need to have some mastery of manipulation in order to get their "fix," whether the fix is of pursuing and catching or simply the glory of someone saying "yes!" to them. I am told it is an intimacy disorder, in which the more vulnerable that they feel in their primary relationship, the more they seek additional sexual connections to bolster their self-esteem.

This book would not be complete if I didn't paint the picture of the circumstances required to beat the odds and recover from sex addiction. Some people estimate the recurrence of sex addiction slips at over 90%. Addictions of any sort have high recurrence rates, because as they say, "once an addict, always an addict." You can choose not to act on your addiction, but you can't stop the desire to do so. Also, it's been demonstrated that sex addiction activates the same neural pathways in the brain as cocaine.

Instead of going to some dealer or liquor store, just think about how a sex addict gets his fix. If he is using hookers, he is continually devaluing human beings for money in order to scratch his itch. If he is persuading people to have sex with him for free, he is continually crossing a moral boundary where he knows that the other person may assume more from the encounter, but he does it anyway. Or he tells himself that it's all in good fun, or in my husband's case, he told himself that he made those women happy. He claimed he "pleasured them", as if he had done them some sort of public service.

Addiction and denial go hand in hand. But in a sex addict's case, demeaning and devaluing another human being's feelings and humanity is required in order for him to get his fix. This is simply not the case with substance abuse. In order for sex addicts to get their fixes, they need to abuse other human beings, instead of substances.

However, a sex addict doesn't see it that way. They will often see their sexual encounters as expressions of "love". Mistaking sex for love is just one of the traits that both sex addicts and their long term partners have in common.

Yes, he had a bad childhood. He is wounded. He is sick. This may be a true statement for all sex addicts. However, don't slip into the false belief that it is some sort of excuse.

Pay attention to how he treats you. Is he respectful? Non-coercive? These are more important qualities to assess than "being nice". Almost all abusers have nice periods. However, the underlying *attitude* and *values* are what drive an abusive partner to be abusive.

Disrespect is inconsistent with love.

Coercion is inconsistent with love.

If you think that your partner is loving, yet he tells you what you *should* think, run away. Anything in the direction of disrespect is an indicator that this person is abusive. Pay close attention to how that person is toward others; if he is disrespectful, do not doubt that he is only pretending to respect you.

Does that sound harsh? Yes, it's a pretty high bar to hit. However, aren't you worth it? How often do you disrespect other people? When you slip up and disrespect someone, do you feel sorry later? Under what circumstances do you believe that it is ok to harm another person, physically or emotionally?

Why would you have any lower standards for your partner than you do for yourself?

Here are the actions I believe I would see if he were truly on a path to recovery:

1. Able to admit fault instead of blaming and denying.
2. Attitude of gratitude, instead of entitlement.
3. Demonstrate he is developing empathy, especially toward his children.
4. Stop the secrets, and the lying.
5. Teach his children how to avoid his fate.
6. Develop the capacity to act lovingly – taking others' best interests to heart.
7. Not use fear, obligation or guilt ("FOG") to manipulate others.

8. Overall, if he were on the path to recovery, instead of bullying, blaming and finger-pointing, he would show compassion toward others, including you.

Trevor is also narcissistic. I believe this is not true of all sex addicts. A predominant trait of narcissists is that they deny reality in exchange for their own world view. That means that, by definition, they do not see other people's points of view. I think narcissists are so insecure and feel so empty inside, they are simply incapable of taking other people's feelings into consideration.

However, how in the whole wide universe did I miss that he was incapable of understanding my feelings? I am still, to this day, flabbergasted. Yes, he is good at hiding, but clearly I wasn't paying attention. I, too, must have been self-absorbed and narcissistic enough to not even notice that he had no capacity to emotionally connect.

Ultimately, I chose Trevor because of his intensity and adventurousness and because I felt comfortable revealing myself to him. Ultimately, that's how he created that net of safety around me that made me feel connected and secure. He listened to my most private thoughts and pretended he understood – or perhaps he just didn't judge those thoughts as crazy. I know that I felt secure in our relationship. I knew that he would never leave me. In fact, he did not.

Narcissists count on the fact that you will feel secure that they'll never leave you. What you don't realize, however, is that they are harmful and toxic. *You need them to leave you*! Ironic, isn't it?

Reprise

What does it mean to move on?

Trevor declares that he has moved on, because he is now remarried. Funny thing, though. No matter where you go, there you are. Moving on has nothing to do with clinging to yet another person. Different person, same old stuff. Trevor clings to human beings like a barnacle on a ship. He's going down, for a second time, and when he feels like he is drowning again, out comes the wallet for the hookers. Or perhaps he never stopped.

I am saddened and disgusted that another woman is being lied to just as I was. However, I feel that my daughter is safer with another woman in the house. I also have been repeatedly counseled by my friends that it's not my place to inform the other woman about Trevor's condition. I don't want to be anywhere near that relationship when/if it blows up. I also don't want my children to think I had anything to do with its demise, because I believe their lives will likely be harder if and when their stepmother is gone.

In any case, I find myself in truly uncharted waters. I am able to live my life now without the constant criticism of my ex, or, since I started this relationship when I was so young, the influence of my mother or father before that. It is exhilarating to be able to make my own decisions, investigate who *I* am, what things *I* like to do, and what *I* want out of life.

I tell people I am still in the "detox" mode, because, among other things, I still occasionally hear echoes of his crazy comments in my mind. For the most part, those are going away. I want to eradicate them completely before I get into a close relationship with the opposite sex. Even before I met Trevor, a prior boyfriend of mine said that I said thank you or was grateful for things that I really should take for granted. He felt that I shouldn't have to thank him for being a decent human being, whether that is opening the door for me, or simply buying a second treat for me at the same time that he bought one for himself. In other words, he wanted me to expect him to be nice to me, and not be so grateful when he did things that he should do anyway.

Is that how it all starts? The cycle of abuse? Get in the mindset in your childhood that any time that the smallest kindnesses are present, you should be extremely grateful? I have always been someone who could say, "Yes, I was in a car accident, but thank God, my son and I were not hurt." There is always something to be grateful about. I'm sure that this a good coping mechanism, but is it so prevalent in my psyche because I have had more hardship than others in my childhood? Perhaps. However, I have also had *fewer* hardships than many.

Moving on does not mean that you jump into another relationship. In fact, jumping into another relationship is a way to re-create what you already had. In that sense it is not moving *on*, but moving *back*. I do feel that I am moving on. I am sailing through the uncharted waters of learning about me. I have no one else to blame for my failures and no one else to praise for my successes. I have to say it's been fabulous to be able to make decisions about what vacations I want to take, what I want to spend money on, what car I buy, where I move, and in general, not have to fight for reason with an illogical human being. The freedom has been fantastic.

The echoes of his psycho comments only get me when I am not conscious of them. I spent the weekend, for example, hanging out by myself and getting some things done that I wanted to get done. I could hear the criticism in my head like a type of pressure, saying "you need to get out" and "look how anti-social you are". Just because I spent the weekend doing exactly what I wanted to do. No one else's input, and no other obligations other than those that I wanted to get done. Feeling like it was "wrong" somehow, because of years of conditioning from a husband who criticized that type of "homebody" behavior. I always was open to doing something else, when he asked. Oh, and I didn't just say I was open to it, he trained me to get in the habit of planning at least one thing so that we could say we did something that weekend.

Now, it's not a bad thing to do something each weekend. What *is* unhealthy is feeling guilty to do what you want, assuming it hurts no one else. In this case, it included exercising each day, taking naps, getting tax information together, and watching football. Why in the world should I feel guilty about that? I felt great at the end of the weekend that I had spent it doing the things that I really wanted to get done and also things that I enjoy. What's all the *guilt* about? Who cares that someone else thinks it's not good enough? Apparently me. Subconsciously, feeling like I am being called a loser. He also thinks people who don't invite other people to their homes for dinner are losers. And somehow that keeps bugging me as well. It's funny, because, the fact of the matter is, my little habits and choices of how I spend my time are just fine. His, on the other hand, that include smoking copious amounts of pot and frequenting hookers, are not.

Yes, I know he had a bad childhood. He was wounded. Something happened that made him this way. However, other people had worse childhoods and somehow came out healthy. My personal opinion is that the only thing that breaks the cycle and makes us grow up is to grapple with, and come to acceptance of, the flaws of our parents. I do not believe that there is a psychologically healthy adult alive who has still unresolved issues with his parents, even if they are 101 years old. I tell my children often that it all starts with your parents, and to truly mature into an adult, it needs to end with your parents as well.

Appendix - Sources for Help

- Checklist of determining if you are in a healthy relationship: <u>Why Does He DO That? Inside the Minds of Angry and Controlling Men,</u> by Lundy Bancroft.

- When people accuse you of something, ask yourself, are they reflecting what they feel themselves? 90% of the time, the reason they say something to you is because it's already in their head. For example, when he says "shame on you," it's because HE feels ashamed! Also, do they say you shouldn't know - do they control the release of information? That is abusive behavior.

- www.COSA-recovery.org

- <u>Mending A Broken Heart</u> by Stephanie Carnes

- www.MarriedToASexAddict.com

- <u>Out Of The Shadows</u> by Patrick Carnes

- <u>Survival Snapshots: Defending Home Against Sex Addiction</u> by Annie Elizabeth Farmer

- Why I Stopped Watching Porn, Ran Gavrieli, TEDxJaffa https://youtu.be/gRJ_QfP2mhU

- You Like Being a Victim: https://youtu.be/ovZA2KQCrXo Gas lighted, again.

- <u>Love is a Choice</u>, Robert Hemfelt, Frank Minirth, Paul Meier

www.ingramcontent.com/pod-product-compliance
Lightning Source LLC
Chambersburg PA
CBHW070133290526
45789CB00005B/2234